Alexander the Great

Jane Bingham

Illustrated by Robin Lawrie

History consultant: Dr. Anne Millard

Series editor: Lesley Sims
Designed by Russell Punter and
Katarina Dragoslavic

First published in 2004 by Usborne Publishing Ltd.,
Usborne House, 83-85 Saffron Hill, London
EC1N 8RT, England.
www.usborne.com

Printed in China.
First published in America in 2005.

Contents

A map of Alexander's world

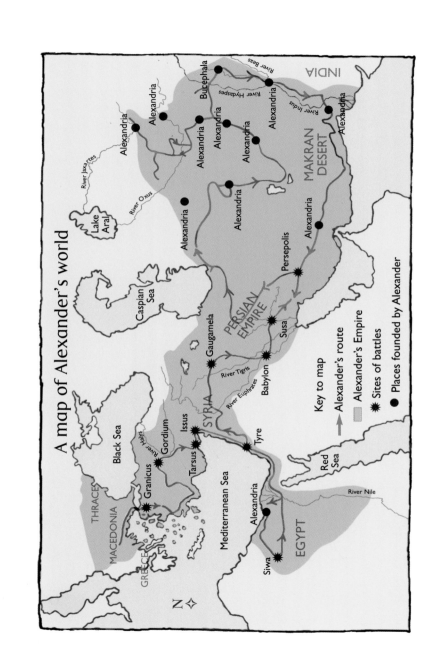

THRACE

MACEDONIA

GREECE

Black Sea

River Halys

Granicus

Gordium

Tarsus

Issus

SYRIA

Tyre

Mediterranean Sea

Red Sea

River Nile

EGYPT

Siwa

Alexandria

Caspian Sea

Lake Aral

River Jaxartes

River Oxus

Alexandria

Alexandria

Alexandria

Alexandria

Alexandria

Alexandria

Bucephala

River Beas

River Hydaspes

INDIA

River Indus

Alexandria

Alexandria

MAKRAN DESERT

Persepolis

PERSIAN EMPIRE

Gaugamela

River Tigris

River Euphrates

Babylon

Susa

Key to map

→ Alexander's route

◼ Alexander's Empire

✳ Sites of battles

● Places founded by Alexander

N

Chapter 1

Prince Alexander

Alexander was born a prince – or so he thought, until his mother, Olympias, shared an incredible secret. His real father, she declared, was Zeus, ruler of the gods. Astounded, Alexander made himself a promise. One day, he vowed, he would rule the world.

As far as everyone else knew, his father was Philip II, ruler of Macedonia, a small, rocky kingdom to the north of Greece. Philip was ambitious and

Olympias was determined. Alexander grew up to be both.

With Philip in charge, and a strong army, Macedonia had grown to twice its size. Philip was building a kingdom to be proud of and he wanted a son fit to rule it.

Alexander's best friend was named Hephaestion and together they learned to fight with all kinds of weapons. Then they put their skills into practice on lion hunts. In rare quiet moments, they played the lyre and read poetry.

As Alexander and Hephaestion reached their teens, Philip hired a famous Greek thinker named Aristotle to teach them. Some days, they discussed science or nature, but on others, Aristotle would fire his pupils' imaginations with tales of mysterious lands far away and the adventures of Greek heroes.

Even though Alexander was inspired by everything, all he really wanted to know was how to rule well.

What makes a good ruler, Aristotle?

To the rest of the court, Alexander was just the prince, until the day he decided he wanted his father's horse.

"If I tame Bucephalus, will you give him to me?" he asked.

"You'll kill yourself!" Philip snapped. Bucephalus was a magnificent horse, but so wild no one dared ride him. Anyone who tried was tossed to the ground and trampled upon.

But Alexander had noticed something nobody else had seen...

Bucephalus was scared of his own shadow. When the horse was led onto the exercise field, Alexander turned it around, so it faced the sun and its shadow fell behind. Then he jumped onto its huge back and galloped across the field. King Philip was so proud of his son he burst into tears.

"I can see Macedonia won't be a large enough kingdom for your talents," he told Alexander, as he gave him Bucephalus.

At just sixteen years old, Alexander was left in charge of Macedonia while his father went off to fight for more land. Philip had barely left before a band of soldiers from Thrace, the kingdom next door, marched in.

This was Alexander's chance to prove himself. Quickly gathering an army, he led his soldiers against the Thracians and beat them easily.

We've thrashed the Thracians.

Hurray!

After that, Alexander and his father led the army together. Even at sixteen, Alexander was always in the thick of the fighting and he never asked a soldier to do anything he wouldn't do himself.

Alexander and Philip made a great team. Soon, they conquered all of Greece. But, while Alexander had grown up respecting his father, they didn't have an easy relationship. Alexander thought his father was much too proud – and he hated the way Philip treated his mother.

Olympias, I've decided to divorce you.

When Alexander was twenty, King Philip decided to marry a new queen. Alexander was furious, but there was nothing he could do. Then, shortly after the wedding, something shocking happened...

Philip was murdered. Alexander immediately put himself forward as the obvious heir. He was strong, handsome, intelligent and, even more significantly, he had huge charm. With the army's backing, he was proclaimed king of Macedonia.

Chapter 2

The young king

Alexander's first act was to give Philip a grand funeral, burying him in a splendid tomb. Then he turned to the question of ruling. Some of the Greeks had already begun to rebel against their new king. Alexander quickly showed them who was boss.

The worst rebels came from the city of Thebes. To teach them a lesson, he flattened their entire city – except for the house of Pindar, a poet. He only spared Pindar because he remembered Aristotle praising him.

Seeing Alexander's ruthlessness, most Greek states submitted to him. But Alexander had bigger plans. For centuries, the Macedonians and Greeks had been sworn enemies of the Persians and Philip had been preparing to invade the Persian Empire just before his death. Alexander was going to carry out his dream.

Over the next year, he trained a vast

army and built up a fleet of ships. With Alexander in charge, and Hephaestion as his second, hundreds of ships set off for the east, carrying not only soldiers, but builders, scientists and artists too.

As they neared the Asian shore, Alexander jumped overboard. Wading through the waves, he hurled his spear into the sand. In one dramatic gesture, he had shown his men he was convinced they would win the land.

Alexander started marching south, planning to conquer the coastal cities, but he soon faced a problem: the vast Granicus River. On the far side, a Persian army was waiting for them. Somehow, Alexander had to cross the river and then attack the Persians.

"It's a tough challenge," commented Hephaestion.

Alexander grinned. "A trickle of water won't stop me!"

Finding the river's shallowest point, he led his men through the rushing water and charged... straight for the Persian general. As one, the Persians turned and ran.

Victorious, Alexander continued south following the coast. Every city he reached, he conquered. Most people treated him as a hero and in the city of Caria, he was greeted by the local ruler, Queen Ada, herself. She came out to meet him carrying a tray piled high with cakes.

Alexander was so impressed, he let her stay on as queen. As they came to know each other better, he began to think of her as a second mother and Ada always gave Alexander and the Macedonians her full support.

In the city of Gordium, Alexander's

attention was caught by a famous chariot. It had stood in the city for years, fastened by a complicated knot no one could untie.

"What's that about?" he asked one of the citizens.

"That chariot is part of an ancient legend," the man replied. "Whoever undoes the Gordian knot will rule Asia." He shrugged. "But it's impossible."

Alexander smiled. Raising his sword in the air, he brought it down and sliced right through the knot.

Chapter 3

Conqueror of the East

"King of all Asia!" he thought, as he marched on. It wasn't going to be easy. By now, Alexander and his forces had been fighting for a year and their food was running low.

"We must make for Syria," he decided, leading the army down a narrow mountain pass. Buoyed up by their victories and with total trust in their leader, the men followed... to find Darius, the king of Persia, waiting for them – with a massive army of six hundred thousand men.

When the Macedonians saw the huge number of Persian soldiers, they were terrified. Caught between mountains on one side and the sea on the other, the situation looked hopeless – until Alexander spotted something. The weakest-looking soldiers on the Persian side all stood together.

Calling over a few of his cavalry, he urged on his faithful horse Bucephalus and charged at the weak spot in the line. As the Persians troops scattered, Alexander galloped for Darius.

The Persian king was in his chariot giving orders when he saw Alexander. Realizing he had no chance of survival, he fled. His shocked army, left without a leader, was defeated with ease.

Alexander, feeling hot and dirty after the battle, strode into Darius's tent for a wash. To his amazement, the tent was crammed with gold and jewels.

"So this is what it means to be a king..." he murmured.

A golden chest gleamed on a table and Alexander took a closer look. "I like that!" he thought. "I think I'll have it for my treasures."

A nervous sigh interrupted his thoughts. Alexander looked up to see several scared faces watching him. When Darius fled, he hadn't just left his gold behind. He'd left his wife, children and mother too.

As Alexander watched, the women fell to their knees in front of the tall soldier who had entered the tent with him.

Please don't kill us, great king!

Sobbing, they pleaded for mercy.

Alexander coughed. "I think you mean me." Appalled by their mistake, the women begged for forgiveness.

Alexander wiped the dirt from his

face and smiled. "It's easily done," he said graciously. "Anyone could mistake my friend Hephaestion for me." He turned and grinned at his second-in-command. "Hephaestion is a great leader too."

With the men refreshed and ready to move on, Alexander went south once more. Again, he attacked and defeated every city he went through. Alexander's confidence and belief in victory spurred on his men, who thought they were unstoppable... until they reached the island of Tyre.

The people of Tyre flatly refused to let anyone into their city. Alexander's generals started muttering among themselves. It looked as if their leader had finally met his match. But Alexander had a plan.

"I want a double-pronged attack," he told his generals. "We'll build a mound in the sea for the siege engines to stand on, and we can attach a ram between two boats."

With the mound built, boulders were lobbed from catapults, blasting through walls already battered by the ram. Soon, soldiers were swarming into the broken city.

The people of Tyre fought fiercely, but finally they had to give in.

When Darius heard that Alexander had even beaten Tyre, he panicked and sent him a message. "Stop fighting now and I'll give you half my lands and my daughter," he offered.

Most of the Macedonians thought this wasn't a bad idea.

Alexander simply laughed and looked squarely at Darius's messenger. "Tell your king I already have half his lands and can marry his daughter anytime I want!" The war wasn't over yet.

Chapter 4

Son of a god?

Alexander's next move was to conquer Egypt. For thousands of years, Egypt had been ruled by a long line of kings, but now the Persians were in charge there too. The Egyptians, who couldn't wait to be rid of them, swiftly made their conqueror their leader.

Soon after he was crowned, Alexander journeyed into the desert. He'd heard of an oasis at Siwa, with a temple to the Egyptian god Amun. Alexander believed Amun and his own god Zeus were one and the same, and he wanted to speak to the temple priest.

Upon his return, he refused to tell anyone what he had asked the priest, or what the priest had said to him. But he did let Hephaestion know he was pleased with what he'd heard. His generals assumed the priest had reassured Alexander he was indeed the son of a god and would conquer the world.

The one thing they all agreed upon was that, after his visit, Alexander grew more arrogant.

While in Egypt, Alexander found a beautiful place by the ocean and decided it was the perfect site for a port. Spreading out parchment, he drew up plans for a city and named it Alexandria. This was only the start. As his conquests continued, he built dozens of cities, all named after him.

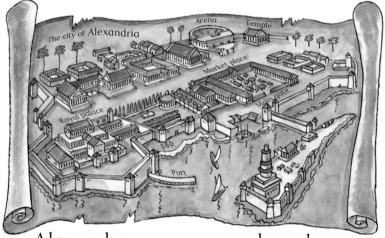

The city of Alexandria · Arena · Temple · Market place · Main gate · Royal palace · Port

Alexander was soon ready to leave Egypt. He was desperate to reach Persia and come face to face with his old enemy, King Darius, once again.

Chapter 5

Clash of the kings

The Macedonians marched for months, searching for Darius. At last, they found him at a place named Guagamela. This time, Darius was sure he could beat Alexander – and he was certainly prepared.

To start with, Darius had chosen a wide battlefield and had the ground completely flattened. His battle plan took account of Alexander's usual battle formation. The Persian army had been well-trained and carried Macedonian-style weapons. Darius even had two hundred chariots with blades on their wheels. But he went further still. As a final touch, he'd scattered spikes on the Macedonians' side of the battlefield, so their horses would stumble when they charged.

The fighting began – and it was ferocious. For once, it seemed the Persians would win. Tasting victory, Darius ordered his chariots to attack. To his horror, instead of fighting back, the Macedonians simply spread out. The Persian horses raced past them and fell on the vicious spikes.

Worse still, the chariots had left a gap in the Persian army, which Alexander charged right through. Racing up to Darius's chariot on Bucephalus, he killed the driver at a stroke.

"Now for the king," he cried, looking around. To his fury, Darius had vanished. Alexander sped from the battlefield the second he could, but he was too late to catch Darius.

I'll get you one day, Darius!

Darius might have escaped, but Alexander had still won an amazing victory. And now he ruled much of the Persian Empire.

Quickly capturing the cities of Babylon and Susa, he began to march east through Persia itself.

The only way forward was through a narrow mountain path known as the Persian Gates. But when Alexander reached the Gates, he found Persian soldiers waiting. He and his army were forced to turn back.

Alexander was enraged, but he was never stumped for long. He simply ordered his men to find someone who knew the area. A local shepherd boy was quickly brought before him. The frightened boy admitted there was another path – over the very top of the mountain.

"But it's too steep and dangerous," the boy said, as he was dismissed.

Alexander didn't care. Being a successful commander meant taking risks. Ignoring the boy's warning, he gathered his commanders together and told them what they had to do.

In the dead of night, with darkness cloaking the mountain, Alexander led a small group of men through the snow and along the second path, to circle around the Persians.

Follow me!

Next morning, as the sun climbed the mountain, Alexander surprised the Persians by attacking from behind, while the rest of his army charged at them from the front. The Persians were trapped and brutally defeated.

Triumphant, Alexander marched on into Persia and soon reached the palace of Persepolis, home of the Persian kings. Gazing at the splendid buildings, Alexander could only think of the thousands of Macedonian soldiers who had died so he could get there.

"The Persians must pay," he decided. "I shall give the palace contents to my soldiers."

Wherever he had conquered, Alexander had, on the whole, been treated as a hero. Now he hoped that the Persians too would welcome him as their king. To his fury, the people shunned him. Alexander was livid.

After a wild party, he ordered his men to set the palace on fire. In one terrible night, Persepolis was burned to the ground.

When he saw the smoking ruins, Alexander regretted his temper.

"Too late now," muttered one of his generals, under his breath.

Leaving the dust and ashes behind, Alexander set off to hunt down Darius. His army marched for four hundred miles in scorching heat, only to find Darius already dead. One of Darius's generals, hoping to please Alexander, had killed the Persian king and dumped his body in a cart for the Macedonians to find.

Alexander was horrified that any man could do such an evil thing to his own king. In disgust, he demanded that the assassin be captured and tried for murder.

Chapter 6

Ruler of Persia

With Darius dead, Alexander was king of the Persians as well as the Greeks – whether the Persians liked it or not. At last, he was fulfilling the promise he made to himself so long ago. But then he started acting like a Persian king. He wore Persian robes and welcomed Persian nobles to court.

The Macedonians were disappointed to see the change in their great leader, who seemed to be distancing himself from them. Things only got worse when he decided he deserved more respect. Persian nobles bowed low to their king and blew him kisses. Alexander ordered the angry Macedonians to do the same.

The Macedonians hated to see their king being so proud. Resentment started to simmer among the troops.

Unaware of the discontent, Alexander held a banquet for his officers. Everyone ate huge amounts of food and drank even more. Made bold by too much wine, Cleitus, one of Alexander's most loyal officers, spoke out.

"Alexander," he observed, "you used to be a soldier like us, but now you act like a Persian king." Putting down his goblet, he went on, "You might think you are the son of a god, but your real father was King Philip and he was a better man than you."

Alexander was incensed. Jumping out of his seat, he grabbed his spear and stabbed Cleitus through the heart.

When he realized what he had done, Alexander broke down in tears. Cleitus was a brave soldier, and he had once saved Alexander's life. For the next three days, Alexander refused to eat. He simply hid himself away and wept.

The news of Cleitus's murder spread and Alexander's men grew scared. From then on, whatever they thought, no one dared say a word against him.

Chapter 7

A royal wedding

Unhappy soldiers were the least of Alexander's worries. Even as king of Persia, there were plenty of leaders eager to challenge him. One of these was Oxartes, ruler of the Scythian tribes who roamed Central Asia.

When Alexander arrived to confront him, Oxartes was waiting, perched high on a mountain. Oxartes was convinced no one would ever reach him. He didn't know Alexander.

Alexander offered a huge reward to the first man to reach the mountain's peak. More than three hundred of his men volunteered.

Later that night, the soldiers started struggling up the rock. Some slipped and fell to their deaths, but many others managed to reach the top.

By dawn, Oxartes was surrounded. He had no choice but to give in and climb down.

I surrender.

The Macedonians were thrilled with their victory and noisily planned a glorious feast. Only Alexander stayed silent. He had noticed a beautiful girl.

She was Roxanne, Oxartes' daughter. When he saw her smile, Alexander fell in love and, a few months later, they were married.

Although Alexander was happy, his men weren't so pleased. In fact, they detested the idea of a foreign queen.

Chapter 8

Into India

Even now he was married, Alexander wasn't ready to settle down. At only twenty-nine, he was ruler of the largest empire in the world – but it still wasn't enough. After all, he had been told he would be king of all Asia. Beyond his Persian Empire lay India, and that was his next target.

His next problem was the Indus river, which blocked the way. The Indus was the widest river the Macedonians had ever seen and no one thought they could cross it.

Rivers had never stopped Alexander in the past and they weren't going to now. Sending some of the men to find small boats, he ordered others to saw up planks of wood. Then he told them to tie the boats together and lay the planks across them.

Of course! A floating bridge.

Alexander jubilantly crossed the Indus, only to meet a more familiar obstacle. A powerful Indian ruler, King Porus, was waiting for him at the next river. And when the army paused at the steep bank of the Hydaspes River, they saw hundreds of trained war elephants on the opposite bank.

The men were terrified until, once again, Alexander came up with a plan.

He knew his army would have no chance in a straight fight. They would have to take King Porus by surprise.

Every morning, the Macedonians began to cross the river and the Indians prepared to fight. But then the Macedonians turned back. King Porus soon became tired and very cross.

Meanwhile, Alexander had sent out scouts, who found another crossing place further upstream. He was ready to make his move.

That night, Alexander marched half his army to the new crossing place and led them over the river. At the same time, the rest of his men started to cross the river as they had so many times before. Porus, tired of the Macedonians' tricks, ignored them.

"Ha! I'm not going to fall for that

again," he snorted.

Soon his army was trapped between two groups of Macedonians – and this time they meant business. In the attack, Porus's elephants panicked and crushed thousands of Indians to death.

Alexander was victorious yet again. Still elated from the battle, he sent a proud message to Porus asking how he wished to be treated.

"Like a king," Porus replied, with calm dignity.

Alexander took him at his word. He appointed Porus as governor of his Indian territories – under Alexander's supreme leadership, of course.

It seemed that Alexander would get whatever he wanted. But he was about to face a terrible blow. Not long after the battle, his beloved horse

Bucephalus died. Alexander was devastated. He had ridden Bucephalus ever since taming him, and they had fought as one in every battle.

Alexander gave his old friend the grandest of funerals. After a rousing ceremony, he built a city at the place where his horse was buried and named it Bucephala. Then he turned his attention to invasions and battles once more.

Chapter 9

The end of the Earth?

Alexander wasn't content with conquering India. He wanted to conquer his way to the very end of the Earth. This horrified most of his men, who realized how big the world was.

"He's crazy," they cried. "We'll be fighting forever and never get home."

Even stories of eastern kingdoms with unimaginable wealth couldn't persuade them. But Alexander insisted. They were going all the way to China.

In India, Alexander had met a wise man who scolded him.

"War is wrong," he told Alexander, "and conquering people is simply a waste of time."

Alexander refused to listen to him. In a last, desperate attempt to show Alexander how strongly he felt, the wise man built a funeral pyre and burned himself to death.

"Don't you see how wrong your actions are?" the old man had begged, as the smoke curled around him.

Alexander had taken no notice and now, set on reaching China, the puny pleas of his troops had even less effect. But the Macedonians were exhausted. They had followed Alexander faithfully, fighting for him for ten solid years, and they missed home.

To make matters worse, the monsoon season had started and all it did was rain...

and rain...

and rain...

The soldiers' swords and shields rusted, their clothes rotted and, on top of all that, they were frequently bitten by snakes seeking dry land. At first, one by one, but then in their tens and hundreds, they pleaded to go home. Alexander just kept on going.

With a grim expression, he led his army across four wide rivers. Some men were swept away and some were eaten by crocodiles. When they reached the fifth river, they refused to go on.

Alexander sulked for three days. He expected unquestioning loyalty and, until now, the men had never refused him outright. But they would not change their minds. In the end, he accepted he would have to turn back.

Chapter 10

Going home

At last, the Macedonians were heading for home. The soldiers were delighted, but their relief was short-lived. An angry Alexander told his generals that he wanted to explore and they would return a different way.

They were led in a brutal march across barren desert. Raging winds blew sand into the soldiers' eyes, the sun blazed down on them and there wasn't nearly enough food and water to go around. Even Alexander didn't have enough to drink. When a soldier did bring him extra water, he poured it away. He wanted to suffer as much as his men.

On the edge of the Makran desert, Alexander split his army into three. Some went by sea, some marched over the mountains, and some followed Alexander into the hostile desert.

It took two months for the Macedonians to cross the desert and thousands of them died in the blistering heat on the way. Less than a quarter of the men who had set out arrived back in Persia.

In the Persian city of Susa, Alexander held a grand wedding for himself to another foreign bride, this time the daughter of Darius. His soldiers weren't happy about it, but they were even less impressed when he announced that he wanted ninety-one of his

officers to marry the daughters of
Persian nobles too.

"We can't be enemies forever,"
Alexander pointed out. "It's asking for
people to turn against us. We must be
allies instead." The officers didn't agree.

"Mixing our cultures will help us
understand each other," Alexander
insisted. Seeing they still weren't
convinced, he showered each couple
with lavish gifts and threw magnificent
parties that went on for days.

When the partying stopped, Alexander had to face the fact that his empire was weakening. While he'd been away from Persia, the governors left in charge had been inciting people against him. He came back to an empire beginning to rebel and had to spend months regaining control.

That autumn, he faced the biggest tragedy of his life. His closest friend and second-in-command, Hephaestion, died. Shattered, Alexander headed for Babylon and shut himself away, refusing to eat.

Desperately unhappy, he shaved off all his hair as a sign of respect for his boyhood friend. Then, almost crazy with grief, he gave orders that every single horse should have its mane and tail cut off too.

Finally, in an attempt to put aside his misery, Alexander started thinking about new invasions. He was still making plans when he went sailing one day with friends. Suddenly, a gust of wind snatched the linen band he wore on his head and carried it away.

Tossed by the wind, the headband came to land on a crumbling building. A priest on the boat shook his head.

"That's the grave of a king," he muttered grimly. "It's a bad sign."

Not long afterwards, Alexander fell sick with a raging fever. On the next day, he went to give orders to his men and collapsed.

"He's going to die," the generals whispered among themselves, and they ordered the soldiers to march past Alexander to say goodbye. By this time, he was too weak to speak, but he raised his eyes to each man as he passed.

That night, a friend bent down to the dying hero. "To whom do you leave your empire?" he asked.

"To the strongest," Alexander whispered. Soon after that, he died. He was just thirty-two years old.

The Macedonians spent a year planning his funeral. Then they laid his coffin in a great golden shrine and set off on the long journey home. But his body never arrived. The coffin was stolen and taken to Egypt by a general who became Ptolemy I.

A few months after Alexander died, his widow Roxanne gave birth to a son. But her plans for him to be king were brutally cut short when they were murdered in a bloody struggle for power. Meanwhile, Alexander's generals were fighting bitterly over his land, and carving it up between them.

In only a few years – far less time than it had taken to build – Alexander's mighty empire had collapsed.

My life of conquest

356BC – I am born. Philip II of Macedonia raises me as his son, but I know my real father is Zeus, king of the gods.

338BC – Philip II conquers Greece – will there be anything left for me to do when I become king?

336BC – I'm proclaimed king after Philip is murdered. At last I have a chance to prove myself.

335BC – The citizens of Thebes rebel against me, so I destroy the city.

334BC – My world conquest begins. My fleet sails to Asia and I win my first battle against the Persians by the Granicus River.

333BC – I come face to face with Darius, King of Persia, at Issus. We win another glorious victory, although Darius escapes.

332BC – Reaching Egypt, I'm treated to a hero's welcome. While visiting the coast, I found my magnificent city of Alexandria.

331BC – Another amazing defeat of the Persians at Guagamela, though Darius gets away again. I march on into Persepolis in triumph.

330BC – Darius dies. (I have nothing to do with it.)

330-328BC – I keep conquering central Asia.

329BC – Angered by his criticism, I kill Cleitus, a loyal officer.

327-326BC – I invade India, defeating King Porus (and all his elephants) on the banks of the Hydaspes River.

326BC – My magnificent horse Bucephalus dies and I establish the city of Bucephela in his memory.

325BC – Plans to conquer China are shattered when my mutinous army refuses to go on. Incensed, I'm forced to turn back.

324BC – Hephaestion, my closest friend, dies. I am devastated.

323BC – *Alexander died suddenly in Babylon aged thirty-two.*